WORDS about Jesus
To help you Worship Him

Carine Mackenzie

Illustrated by Chad Thompson

CF4·K

God the Son
(John 3:16)

Jesus is the Son of God and has always existed. He has never had a beginning and will never have an end. He has always been with God the Father and God the Holy Spirit.

The Bible tells us that there is only one God but there are these three different persons in this one God – Father, Son and Holy Spirit.

We are all born sinners. We go against God and do, say and think wrong things. Sin has to be punished by a just God. We need a Saviour. God knows our need. God loves to be merciful and kind. God the Father sent his Son to this world to be the Saviour of sinners.

God's Life never began, but when did your Life begin?

This holy one called the Word became a man, was born into this world as a baby and grew up to be an adult. But he never stopped being God the Son.

Jesus is God and man. This is an amazing mystery for us to believe. We should worship God – we should praise him. We should tell him and others how wonderful he is.

What do you think the baby in the picture needs? Jesus was born as a baby too – just like you – but he never sinned.

'You will have this child by the special power of the Holy Spirit.'

Mary was troubled and afraid at this news. But the angel reassured her. 'Do not be afraid Mary, for you have found favour with God.' Mary was content with the news about her coming baby. She worshipped the Lord God.

Which student has won the most high grade? God is the most high, the most powerful and the most wonderful. He knows everything!

Jesus the Baby
(Matthew 1:21, Luke 2:7)

Jesus was born in very humble circumstances. Perhaps you were born in a hospital or even in your own home. Jesus was born in a stable. Mary and her husband Joseph had to travel to Bethlehem on the order of the government, to be registered.

The town was busy with other visitors. There was no room at the inn. They were given a place to rest in a stable. There the baby was born. Mary wrapped him up in a blanket and laid him in a manger.

The baby was given the name 'Jesus' which means 'God is the Saviour', because he would save his people from their sins.

Do you know anyone else with your name? Why was Jesus given his name? What is being rescued in this picture? Who does Jesus save or rescue?

Christ
(Luke 2:11, Isaiah 61:1)

After Jesus was born, an angel appeared to shepherds looking after their sheep in a field near Bethlehem. The angel brought wonderful news for them and all people, 'The Saviour who is Christ the Lord has been born tonight in Bethlehem.'

Christ was the Greek word meaning 'anointed one' — the one set apart by God for a special task. The Jewish people called this person the Messiah. They were looking forward to his coming which had been promised in the Old Testament.

Have you ever been given a special task to do? You are given it because someone trusts you to do it. We can trust Jesus to save us. He did all that was needed to be done!

Saviour
(Matthew 1:21, Romans 5:6)

Do you know what your name means? The name Jesus means 'God is the Saviour'. Before Jesus was born an angel told Joseph to give that name to the baby.

Jesus would save his people from their sins when he died for them on the cross.

Sin deserves punishment from a just and holy God. Jesus took that punishment for those who repent and trust in him. Instead of punishment they receive forgiveness and eternal life.

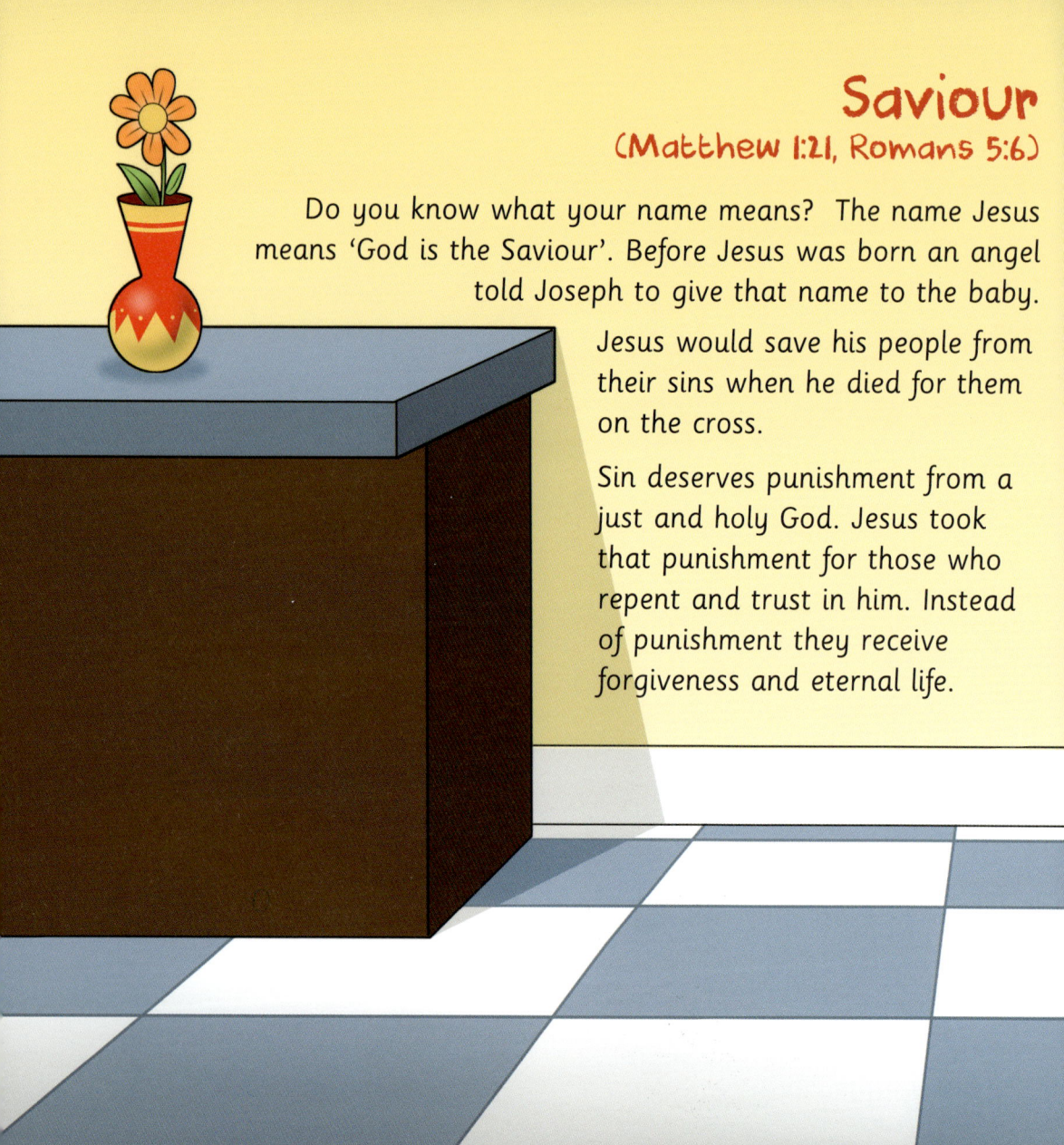

Redeemer
(John 8:36)

If a person was kept as prisoner, it could be possible to set them free with a payment of money. This is called 'redeeming'. The person who paid the price is a redeemer.

Jesus is called the Redeemer. He paid the price for sin. This delivers his people from slavery to sin. The price he paid was not money, but his death on the cross. This great price bought our freedom.

Have you ever saved your money for something special? Jesus paid a great price to save his people from sin. It wasn't money – what was it?

Prophet
(Hebrews 1:1-2, John 16:13)

In the Bible there are many books written by prophets – Isaiah, Jeremiah, Hosea, Joel and others. These men were instructed by God to tell people what his will was for the present and the future.

Jesus is the great Prophet. Through his Word and Spirit, we are taught about God, about our sin and about God's great plan of salvation.

In the past God spoke through his prophets. Now he speaks through his Son, the Lord Jesus. We must listen to his Word and be guided by his Spirit.

Words are important. Where in your house can you see words? How often do you speak? God speaks through his Word, the Bible.

Priest
(Hebrews 4:14, Hebrews 7:25)

An Old Testament priest would offer sacrifices in the temple and pray for the people. That was his job. Jesus offered himself as the perfect sacrifice for sin once and for all.

Jesus is in heaven now, praying continually for his people. He is our Priest. We may forget to pray, but Jesus never forgets.

What have these boys forgotten to take with them on their walk? One of them seems to have lost something? What is that?
Jesus is not absent-minded.
He remembers you.

King
(1 Timothy 6:15, Philippians 2:9-10)

Jesus is the King of kings – the greatest ruler of all. His kingdom consists of all God's people. He rules wisely and fairly. He gives us good laws to guide us and keep us from harm. He defends his people from Satan, the evil one.

The Bible tells us that every knee will bow one day at the name of Jesus. God has given him the name that is above every name.

When you play 'Let's pretend' what do you want to be? God doesn't pretend to be King as he rules everything. He is perfect. He is the best.

Mediator
(1 Timothy 2:5)

Sometimes when two people have a serious disagreement, they need a third person who understands them both, to come and help them to make peace. This person is a mediator or go-between.

Jesus is the mediator between God and people. We, as sinners, have offended the holy God. Because Jesus is both God and man, he is the only one who can deal with this problem.

As a man he could take our place and bear our punishment. As God he was the perfect sacrifice. So Jesus was able to make peace between God and people.

Who is being the mediator in this picture? He is trying to solve the problem between two other boys. Jesus is the mediator between God and his people.

Creator
(John 1:1, Mark 4:39)

In the beginning God created the heaven and the earth. He spoke the Word and the sea and land, plants, animals and man were all created.

Jesus is known as the Word. 'In the beginning was the Word and the Word was with God and the Word was God' (John 1:1). Jesus who is God the Son, the Creator, has power over his creation. He spoke to the wind and it ceased. He spoke to the sea and it became calm.

If you were in a spaceship you would see stars and planets. God has made these. What have you made? Is anything you make as good as what God does? Look at a leaf then a star. God did that!

Bread of Life
(John 6:35)

When we are hungry, we love to eat a sandwich or a piece of toast. That satisfies our hunger. Everyone has a longing that needs to be satisfied. This longing is like hunger or thirst. Our spirits or souls long for a satisfaction that possessions and money cannot bring. Fame or success can't bring it, friends and family cannot give it either.

The only satisfaction for this longing is to be found with the Lord Jesus. Jesus himself told us that he is the Bread of Life.

When you are hungry, what food do you like best? What's your favourite sandwich? When your soul is hungry who is it hungry for?

Door
(John 10:9)

The safe and proper way to enter a house is through the door. A thief might try some other way, like a window.

Jesus said that he was like a door of a sheepfold. That door was the way that a sheep entered the place of safety. Anyone going in to the sheepfold by another way was up to no good. Only through Jesus, do we have access to God the Father. Only through Jesus, will we receive forgiveness of our sins and gain access to heaven at last.

There is a door on this barn and a window - where are they? How many doors are there into your home? Jesus is the only way to God the Father.

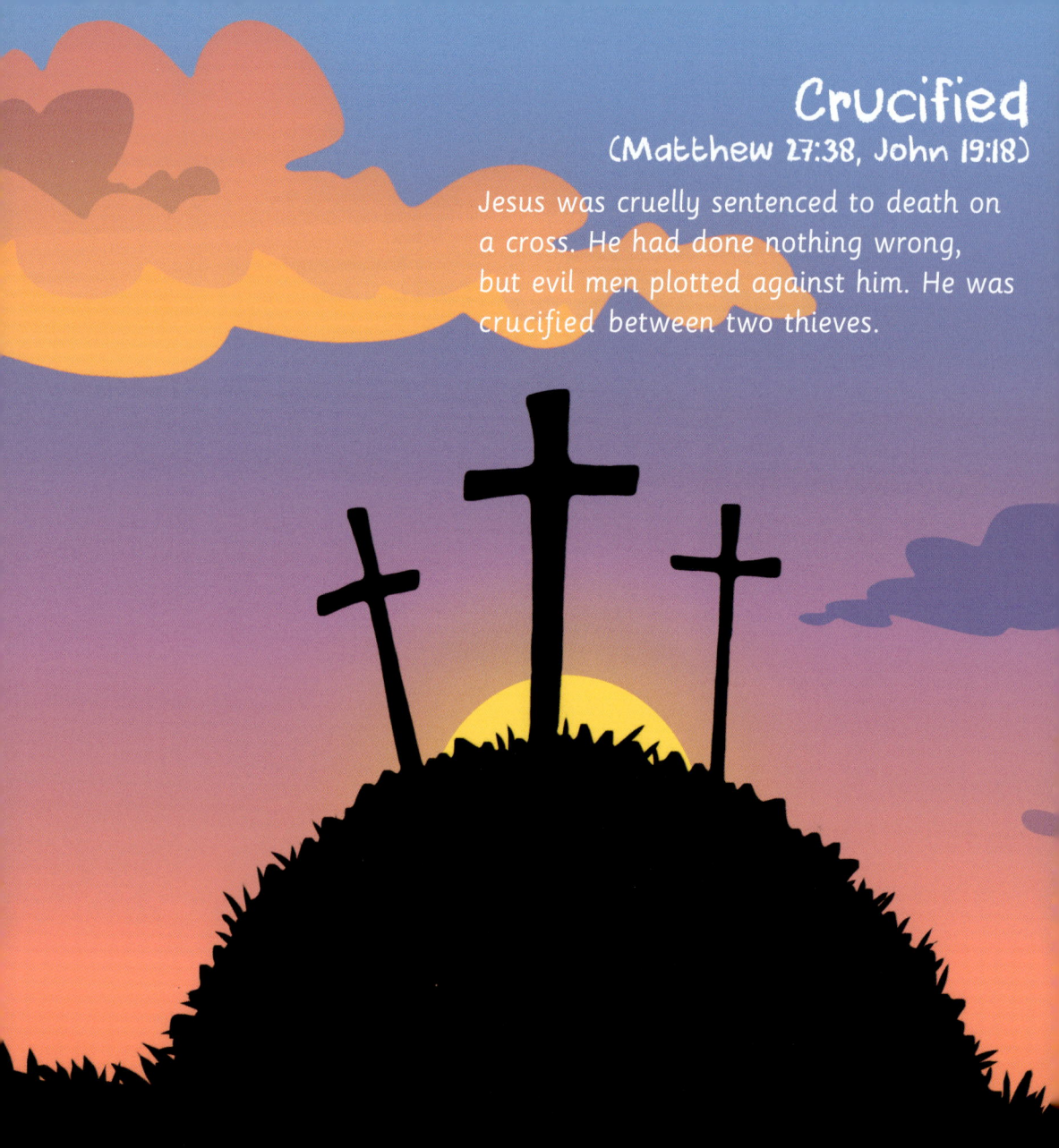

Jesus knew all along that this would happen. His suffering and death were the punishment for the sins of his people. He took their place. He did it willingly. He took the full weight of the just anger of God on himself so that those who trust in him would be saved.

When you win a race are you glad? When you win a prize what do you get? Jesus died on the cross. This was not a defeat, it was a victory. Read the next bit of the book and you will understand why.

Risen
(Luke 24: 1-10)

The Lord Jesus Christ conquered death. His body was buried in a tomb but he did not remain there. When some women came to see where he was buried, they found that the stone had been rolled away. Two angels in dazzling clothes told them, 'Jesus is not here. He has risen.'

Jesus was alive. Sin and death had been beaten by God's wonderful power. Many people saw the risen Lord Jesus in the days following. They were witnesses to the fact of the resurrection. Jesus really did rise from the dead.

When you get up in the morning what do you do first? What has happened in your world before you wake up? God has power over all life. Jesus even conquered death!

Ascended
(Luke 24:50-53, Acts 1:9-11, John 16:13, John 14:3)

What happened next? Jesus was carried up into heaven as his disciples watched. They gazed up to heaven as he ascended through the clouds. They worshipped him, knowing that he was God.

Jesus had told his disciples that he would leave them to go back to his Father, God. But he told them that he would send his Holy Spirit to be with them to help and comfort them, and guide them into all truth.

Jesus also promised that he would return one day to the earth. And as the disciples stood gazing after Jesus, two angels came and reminded them of what Jesus had promised. 'Jesus who has been taken into heaven will come back again the same way that you have seen him leave.'

They were joyful and returned to Jerusalem worshipping Jesus and blessing God.

When you know a friend is coming to visit what do you do? Are there special foods you get ready, or games? Are you happy and excited? We should rejoice that Jesus is coming back one day!

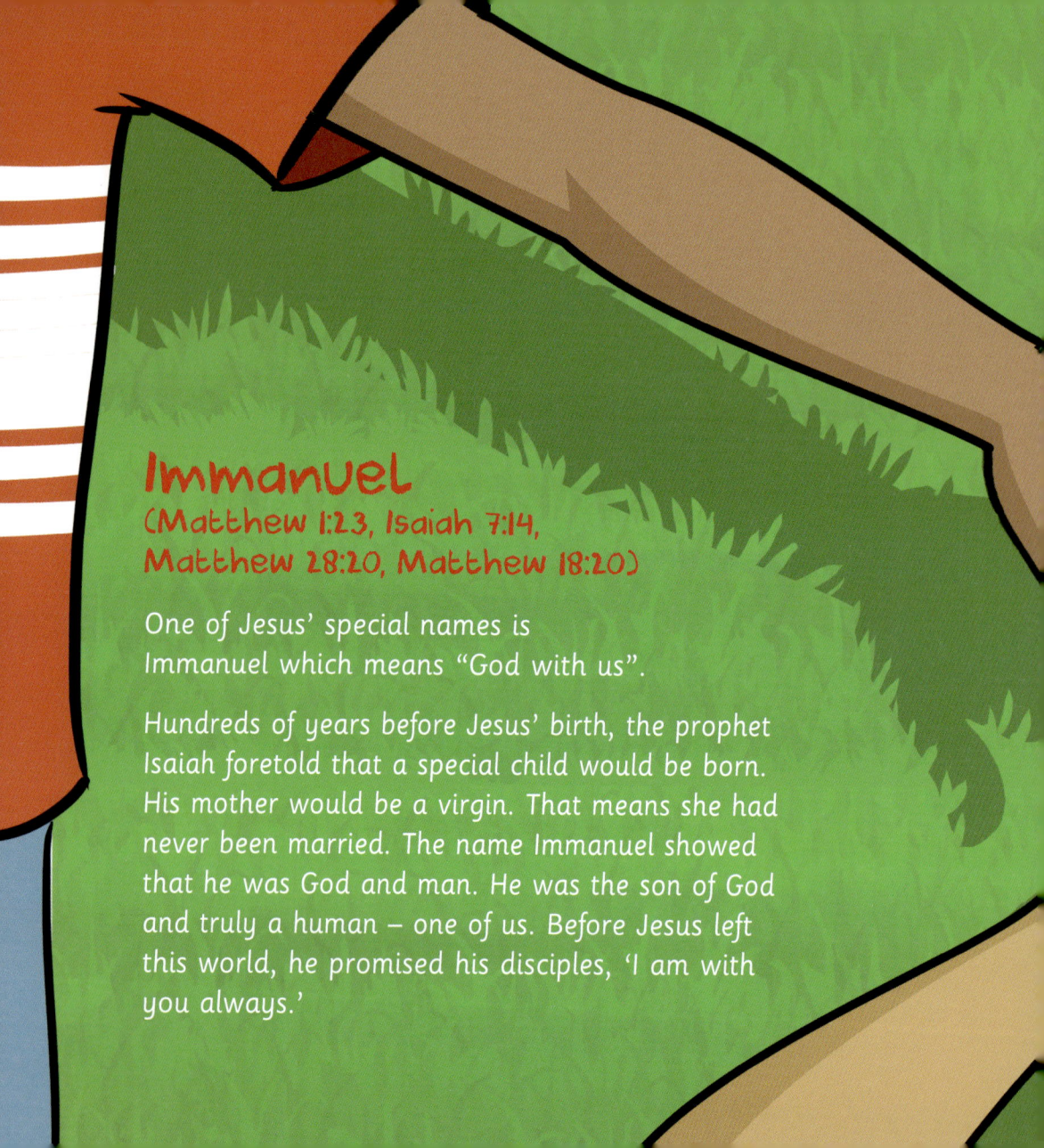

Immanuel
(Matthew 1:23, Isaiah 7:14, Matthew 28:20, Matthew 18:20)

One of Jesus' special names is Immanuel which means "God with us".

Hundreds of years before Jesus' birth, the prophet Isaiah foretold that a special child would be born. His mother would be a virgin. That means she had never been married. The name Immanuel showed that he was God and man. He was the son of God and truly a human – one of us. Before Jesus left this world, he promised his disciples, 'I am with you always.'

Friend
(Matthew 11:19, Matthew 19:13–15, Proverbs 18:24)

Jesus cares for the poor and needy. He has a concern for those we might think are not very important.

Sometimes Jesus was criticised for spending time with sinners. 'He is a friend of tax collectors and sinners,' they said.

Jesus is also a friend of children. When some mothers brought their children to meet Jesus, the disciples tried to turn them away. But Jesus said, 'Let the children come to me. Don't turn them away.' He took them in his arms and blessed them.

Jesus is the best friend anyone could have. He is the friend who sticks closer than a brother.

What do you like to do with your friends? How is Jesus your friend?

Shepherd and a Lamb
(John 10:11, John 1:29)

A shepherd looks after his sheep. Sheep need food and water. They need protection from wild animals. Jesus loves and cares for all those who follow him. He teaches them with his Word, the Bible. He protects them from evil. He gives them rest for their souls.

When John the Baptist saw Jesus he said, 'Behold the Lamb of God who takes away the sin of the world.'

If we have faith in Jesus, he will take away our sin and make us clean in God's sight.

When you wash your hands do they always stay clean? Is there ever a day when you don't disobey God? Who can help? Who takes away your sin?

Light of the World
(John 8:12)

'I am the light of the world,' said Jesus. 'If you follow me you will not walk in darkness, but have the light of life.'

Light removes the dark. It guides and helps us to follow the right path. Jesus, the Light, gets rid of the darkness of sin and evil. He shows us our sin and guides us to repent and look to him for forgiveness.

The light from a lighthouse warns you of dangerous rocks. Jesus and his Word warn us of the danger of sin, so we can avoid the harm it causes.

Teacher
(Matthew 7:28-29, Luke 11:1-4)

Jesus was an amazing teacher. People knew that he spoke with great power and authority. Jesus taught using stories, called parables. These stories told about everyday events like sowing seed or building a house, but they also taught a lesson about God's kingdom. Only those who trusted in God would understand the true meaning.

His disciples asked Jesus to teach them to pray. So Jesus taught them the prayer we know as the Lord's Prayer. We can use this prayer that Jesus taught too.

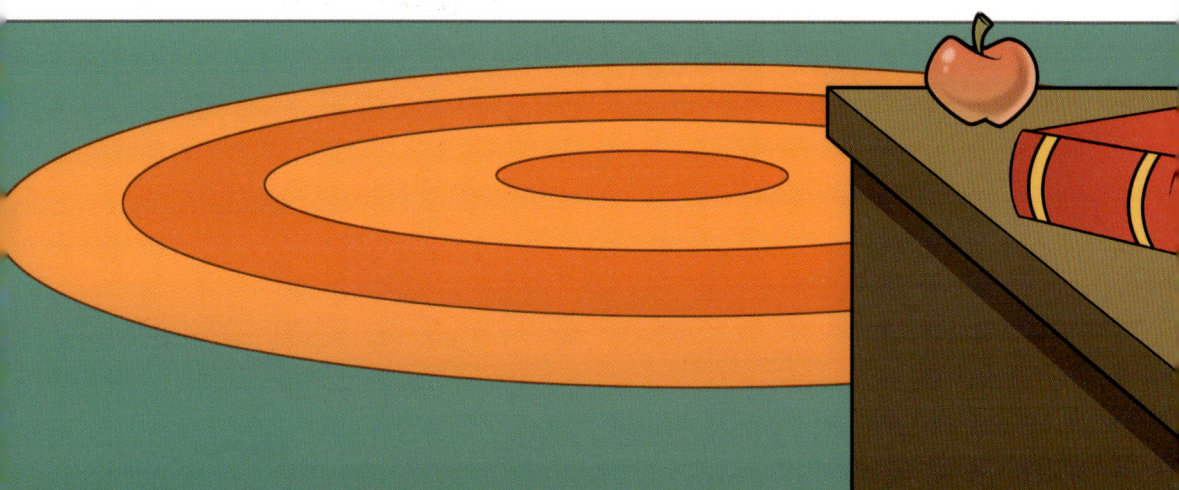

Truth
(John 14:6, Exodus 20:16)

All that Jesus ever said is true because he is truth. 'I am the way, the truth and the life,' he said. 'No one comes to the Father except through me.'

He never told a lie. He never tried to deceive. He kept all the commandments perfectly, including the ninth which tells us not to lie or say untruths about others.

We often sin by telling lies and saying wrong and hurtful things. Jesus' death on the cross cleanses his people from sin. He gives them his righteousness as a covering.

We might use our words and mouth to disobey God. How can we use our mouth and words to please God?

Healer
(Luke 9:11)

The Lord Jesus showed his power over disease and disability. Many sick people came to him and he healed them.

What bit of the boy is this doctor looking at? Thank God for hospitals and the way he uses doctors and nurses to heal people.

He made a blind man see, a lame man walk and a dumb man speak. Lepers were cleansed of their disease. A little girl aged twelve was even raised from the dead.

Jesus was the great healer and he still is. All healing comes from God. When we recover from a cold or an injured leg, we should thank the Lord, who is the great healer. The big disease that needs healing is sin. Jesus provided the cure when he bled and died on the cross. If we trust in him, our disease of sin will be healed.

Head of the Church
(Colossians 1:18, Revelation 5:9)

Jesus loves the church. The church is the people of God, not the building where the church meets. Every day people come to trust in Jesus and so become part of the church.

Jesus is the head of the church – leading and guiding his followers. Jesus cares for his church and builds it up. His church is all over the world. People from every tribe and language and nation are part of it.

How many different countries do you know? What different languages do they speak? Thank God for his Word, the Bible.

Ni Hao!

Way to God
(John 14:6)

There is only one way to come to God and be in heaven at last. The Lord Jesus is the way. 'I am the way,' he said. 'No one comes to the Father except through me.'

If we trust in Jesus we have never-ending life. If we believe he is the only way, our sins will be forgiven and we will one day be in heaven with Jesus for ever.

Pick a place on the globe. How would you travel there? There are many different ways to make journeys. But there is only one way to heaven. How do we get there?

Prince of Peace
(Isaiah 9:6, Philippians 4:6-7, Hebrews 12:3)

Sometimes we feel anxious and worried. The Lord Jesus tells us to take all our cares to him in prayer with thanksgiving. He has promised to give us his wonderful peace to guard our hearts and minds.

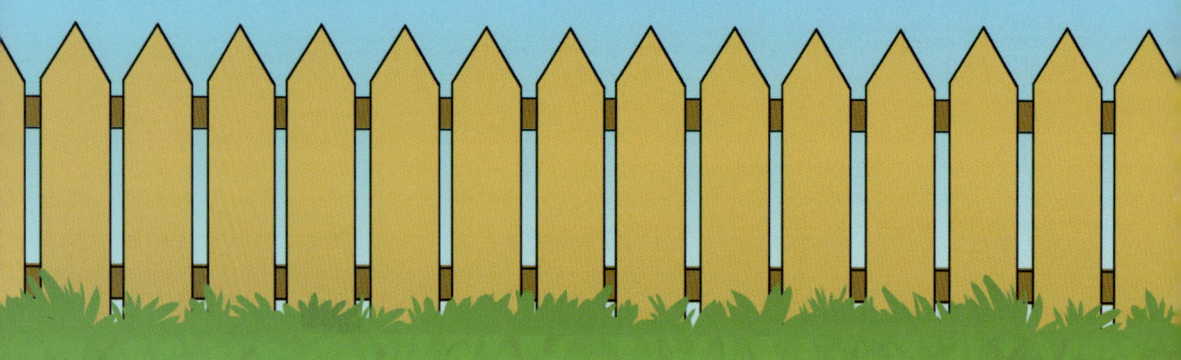

Jesus is called the Prince of Peace. Through trusting in him, we have safety and security in every situation. Thinking about Jesus and what he has done for us, brings peace to our hearts.

What items are there in this picture to give the girl safety? Jesus gives us safety by saving us from our sin and bringing us to heaven to be with him.

10 9 8 7 6 5 4 3 2 1
Copyright © Carine Mackenzie 2020
ISBN 978-1-5271-0614-7
Published in 2021
by Christian Focus Publications, Ltd.
Geanies House, Fearn,
Ross-shire, IV20 1TW, Scotland.
www.christianfocus.com

Illustrations by Chad Thompson
Printed and bound by Gutenberg, Malta
Scripture version: Author's own paraphrase

Our glorious God is honoured by the praises of little ones (Psalm 8:2). Jesus Christ welcomed the children, and He used everyday things to communicate deep spiritual truths. This wonderful book will help you teach small children to know and love and praise the Savour.
(Sharon James, author and speaker)

Children need to learn the deep truths of the Bible and included in that is learning the character of Jesus. This simple book carefully teaches who Jesus is and what we learn of Him from Scripture in a child-friendly manner; with Scripture references, relatable pictures, and discussion questions for each attribute of Jesus. Every parent needs this book to help them guide their children in a greater understanding of who Jesus is, leading to worship.
(Bethany Darwin, author of *Sing and Play Big Bible Truths*)

All rights reserved. No part of this publication may be reproduced, stored in a retrieval system, or transmitted, in any form, by any means, electronic, mechanical, photocopying, recording or otherwise without the prior permission of the publisher or a licence permitting restricted copying. In the U.K. such licences are issued by the Copyright Licensing Agency, Copyright Licensing Agency, 4 Battlebridge Lane, London SE1 2HX.